D0412478

Bill Beaumont
BEDSIDE RUGBY

Bill Beaumont
REDDY
BUSH

Bill Beaumont
BEDSIDE RUGBY

Illustrations by Edward McLachlan

Fontana/Collins

First published by William Collins (Willow Books) 1986
First issued in Fontana Paperbacks 1987
Second impression October 1987
Third impression November 1987

Copyright © in text Bill Beaumont 1986
Copyright © in illustrations Lennard Books 1986

Made by Lennard Books
Mackerye End, Harpenden
Herts AL5 5DR

Editor Michael Leitch
Designed by Pocknell & Co.
Production Reynolds Clark Associates Ltd

Printed and bound in Great Britain
at the University Printing House, Oxford
by David Stanford, Printer to the University

Conditions of Sale
This book is sold subject to the condition
that it shall not, by way of trade or otherwise,
be lent, re-sold, hired out or otherwise circulated
without the publisher's prior consent in any form
of binding or cover other than that in which it is
published and without a similar condition
including this condition being imposed
on the subsequent purchaser

CONTENTS

NUMBERED FOR LIFE

Rugby is a running game, but not everyone travels at the same speed. No-one knows this better than the schoolmaster in charge of the beginners' class. It is September, and thirty boys aged eight and nine stand shivering before him on the edge of a windswept field. The annual casting session is about to begin.

The schoolmaster has learned to be quite ruthless in his task of selection. If Nature had not given him a helping hand by moulding boys in several distinct shapes, his job would be a lot more difficult. Fortunately, Nature has done her bit more than adequately with this year's intake and he knows he would be a mug not to take full advantage.

Seconds later, the four tallest boys have become second-row forwards. For life. Next come the props. The four fattest boys, also presumed the slowest, are appointed. They seem delighted, within the limits of their intelligence, and immediately retire to one side and start butting each other.

Now it gets harder, because the master in charge is looking for ball-players he can turn into half-backs, but he has little to go on except for the brief kickabout he allowed before the squad lined up. Two or three boys had looked vaguely promising, he remembers, and on the further basis that they are of average height and build, they are told to be scrum-half or stand-off. Another boy who was seen to catch the ball when someone punted it to him becomes one of the full-backs. The other is the boy who punted it.

Next the master chooses his wingers. This he does by a slightly different process,

Sorry....Wibley....but....we....need....one....more....tall....boy....for....a....second....row....forward.

which involves a subtle piece of applied psychology. The boys he picks are undoubtedly the biggest weeds in the group; every one, physically, is a broken reed – snivelling, knock-kneed, spiritless, arms clutched across his puny chest to keep out the wind, eyes staring down wetly and with extreme distaste at the alien grass. All four look perfect for the part, and the master has to hope that there are no freaks among them who really would like to play rugby. For this is the critical point: these boys have been turned into wingers because it is assumed that they hate the whole idea of the game and, in time, when they have learned to cope with the extreme loneliness out there on the touch-line, will feel only gratitude that no-one wants to give them a pass, and at the same time admire the beautiful symmetry of playing opposite a boy of equal weediness who will never need to be tackled.

Seventeen or eighteen boys have now been placed in the field and given a mission in life. The rest are pushed in around them like pieces of temporary filler, and now the boys are ready for their first taste of the real thing.

Before this first game is fifteen minutes old, the pattern of play for the rest of the season has become established. To the inexperienced viewer it looks like a swarm of bees buzzing everywhere in a kind of cloud formation, but the master in charge has already noticed that within the cloud three, possibly four, boys are running the whole thing. They make all the long runs with the ball, zig-zagging across the field; they score the tries, attempt the conversions, take the free-kicks and, from time to time, tackle each other. They are the enthusiasts, the ball-players. In contrast to them, about half the boys in each team have begun to demonstrate clearly that they do not want to know about rugby and its complicated apparatus, the senseless running and the painful and sometimes smelly physical contact, the rain, the mud, the wind – in fact, the sheer barbarity of it, when all the time they could be snug and warm indoors somewhere, watching a video.

Are you holding back, boy?

PARENTS AND OTHER DIFFICULTIES

The master in charge realizes that this is all quite normal and an essential part of the settling-down phase. The good ball-players can now be moved, if necessary, to their final positions on the field, where with a bit of luck they will remain for the next twenty or thirty years. He is careful, too, not to write off all the stragglers. Some of them may still turn out to be adequate, even quite useful players. At this stage in their careers they may be holding back for one of several reasons.

The first of these reasons is simple confusion. They don't understand the rules. I can remember this problem all too clearly. When I started playing, at a prep school in Kirkby Lonsdale, we played rugby in one winter term and soccer in the other; so that was a double ration of rules we had to learn and master. On my first day on the rugby field, at the age of nine, I was immediately typecast as a heavy and set to play prop forward.

Now, I'd seen the odd game of rugby, and my father and grandfather had played in their time, but I hadn't a clue about the actual positions and what they meant. After I'd played a few games, it came as a great surprise to me to learn that forwards could score. The way I'd worked it out, the forwards got the ball and passed it to the backs who did all the scoring. 'No, no', someone said, 'you can score as well.' 'Oh,' I thought, 'well, that's worth knowing.'

Then there's offside. The offside laws in rugby are complicated enough to give international referees a headache, and they can have a crushing effect on nine-year-old beginners who simply can't see where they've gone wrong. It's not like soccer, where players can pass the ball forward whenever they want and go more or less where they like on the field. It takes a long time for some lads to see that rugby is different and that you have to be behind the ball in the direction you are playing.

Another problem that boys may have to contend with is their parents. I see them today at mini-rugby matches, standing on the touch-line and screaming at little Jimmy to 'pull his ears off' and getting really uptight if he doesn't. I suspect that some of them are trying to relive their own youth through their son, and it doesn't always work for the simple reason that some little Jimmys are more concerned about the fact that they are cold and wet-through than with the course of the game; they can't wait to get off the field and into the showers and claim their bottle of Coke and packet of crisps.

Some parents, also well-meaning uncles and family friends, enjoy the business of typecasting future rugby players when they are still in their prams. The funny thing is, they invariably say the boy will be a prop. 'Look at the size of him,' they say. 'A good thick neck like that – he's got to be a prop!' I am speaking here from personal experience, because now it's happening with my young lads. People who see them only have to take one look – and another prop is born!

Mummy's very, very proud of you, Jimmy.

THE BIG TIME BECKONS

Back with the under-tens, it is soon time for the master in charge to pick a team to play against another school. Not an easy task. As he well knows, he has thirty players, but only about a dozen want to play; of these, only six or seven show any promise, so the team will be the usual cocktail of stars, makeweights and no-hopers, several of whom will be playing under duress.

I actually have quite a lot of sympathy for small boys who don't like being forced to play rugby. Where my school played, up in the wilds of Westmorland, it was always throwing it down and freezing cold. To be made to stand out on the wing, shivering, against your will, must have been purgatory. An added hazard were the cowpats. We played on a field which was more often used by cows than schoolboys, and it was quite a feat of memory to note in your mind where the cowpats were so you could avoid visiting that part of the pitch.

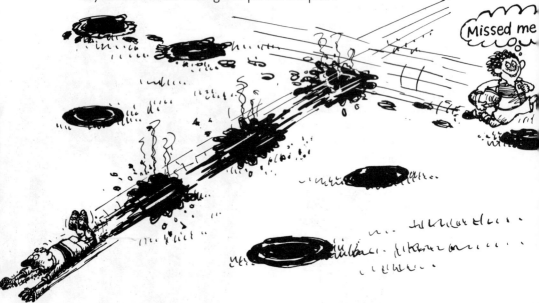

In the forwards it wasn't so bad. We were already developing the kind of comradeship that forms among the muddiest, grubbiest boys. We didn't welcome the cowpats, but at least there was a chance with us that if we did hit one nobody would notice the difference.

I also had an extra piece of equipment which I regarded as a great status symbol. My ears had been getting sore and I must have written home about it because one day my father sent me a scrum cap. I loved it. I loved waltzing about with this yellow thing on the top of my head; I thought I was the complete bees' knees. Looking back, the scrum cap may well have done me some good, especially against other schools who didn't know me. In those days, owning a scrum cap was a bit special, therefore a useful aid in overawing opponents who might think to themselves: 'Crikey, he's got a scrum cap. He must be good.'

It's ironic that scrum caps have virtually faded from view today, because players became convinced that the possibility of being garotted with one was a greater danger than having their ears ripped off without one.

If the school has reasonable success, or even if it doesn't, the same settling-down process continues until all fifteen positions in the team are fixed. Provided no-one is expelled, or a brilliant new boy arrives, this year's Under-10s become next year's Under-11s, moving up each year until they reach the 1st XV.

The position of hooker is subject to more experiment than most. This is now a much more responsible position than it used to be because the hooker has to throw the ball in as well as hook it back in the scrum. The modern hooker therefore needs more in the way of ball skills – to throw the ball in straight *and* to the agreed man in the line-out – as well as brainpower – to remember the signals – than his old-fashioned counterpart. At schoolboy level the hooker doesn't have to be big, in fact a lot of boy hookers are quite spindly. What is more important is that he should be able to swing for the ball between the two props. Much time at prep schools and similar establishments can be spent testing the various candidates for hooker. Usually the winner is the one who can hang there like a chimp *and* get his foot to the ball when it comes into the scrum.

This is no easy skill to acquire, and partly explains why the front row develop a close inter-personal relationship among themselves, sometimes to the exclusion of team-mates and anything happening elsewhere on the field. After a while they aren't bothered if their side loses the game by 20 points; if at the same time they got three heels against the head, that counts as three-nil – a victory!

We're still looking for a wing forward, Withington....

If the master in charge finds himself still looking for a wing forward, his best bet is to select the biggest misfit in the year and stick him in as open-side wing forward. As soon as the boy realizes that he is being given *carte blanche* to be the chief wrecker and do everything that he gets punished for doing in ordinary life, he will instantly blossom and flourish and become an indispensable member of the team. The master's main problem is then to make sure the boy is available for matches – even if it means somehow bailing him out of detention and lying through his teeth to other members of staff.

SOME THINGS THAT NEVER CHANGE

At the beginning of this chapter I mentioned that not all rugby players travel at the same speed. Another strange but undeniable characteristic of schoolboys is that they do not grow at the same speed. Some, after a great leap at puberty, stop growing altogether – with confusing results all round.

When he is thirteen or so, this boy is nicknamed something like 'Tank' and other boys look up to him. The master in charge has no hesitation in putting him in the second row where his brute force

works wonders. In broken play, too, he is a great success, and quite unstoppable if he is given the ball within ten or fifteen metres of the try-line. Opponents can attach themselves to any part of his legs or body, he will still drag them all with him and get the touch-down.

This is fine for the first few years, but then someone notices that two or three other boys are catching up in size with Tank, and he doesn't seem to be responding. What's more, Tank's old trick of getting the ball and rumbling regardless for the try-line doesn't seem to be working so well. While this is going on, Tank's attitude towards the game begins to change. At this stage it is essential that the master in charge understands what is happening and tries to remotivate Tank to play for the team. If he succeeds, Tank can still make a useful contribution, especially if he can be induced to run faster (something he never considered important before). If he lets Tank go, the boy will rapidly degenerate into a lemonade-swilling, toffee-guzzling mess with no future at all, not even as a touch-judge.

A less distressing, though apparently incurable feature of rugby at the under-ten level is the total absence of a place-kicker. Boys volunteer for the job, of course, since the reward for success is huge in terms of prestige, but all their herculean efforts fail to add a single point to the score-sheet.

With ordinary free-kicks the absence of a kicker can be concealed by a steady policy of touch-kicks broken by deft use of the tapped penalty and massed charges for the line (a kind of flying wedge with holes in). However, after a try is scored there is no ducking the challenge of the conversion. The kick must be taken and all the rituals observed – placing the ball, grass in the wind, the measured steps back, the glare at the posts and the deep breath taken, the rush at the ball and the boot drawn back, then the kick itself and the ball sent *flying*....about four yards, and most of that along the ground.

It would be heartbreaking to watch these young place-kickers if the boys themselves actually minded very much. But most seem to accept that they must serve a pretty barren apprenticeship until they are about thirteen years of age. Then, if they have practised enough and grown strong enough, the day will dawn when they get one over. After that, there will be no holding them.

HIGHLIGHTS AND MENTAL REPLAYS

To play bedside rugby reasonably well, it helps if you have quite a good memory. When a guy stops playing, he can still watch games involving other people, but these never seem to have quite the same charm as the games in which he himself featured – and occasionally, perhaps, did something useful. Unfortunately, none or very few of these career highlights gets recorded on video, and so he has to resort to memory and to mental replays.

It could be worse: at least no-one is going to complain if he tastefully edits one or two moments to his own advantage. All his mates are doing just that; he can tell from the way, down at the clubhouse, they retell the old stories, each time slightly adapting them.

In my own case, although I played in a lot of matches at club level and higher, I find that memory is a good historian because somehow it manages to file all the truly outstanding memories ahead of the rest, even though they may come from very different periods in my playing career.

The whole Grand Slam year of 1980 remains fresh in my mind – not surprisingly – but the sharpest moments of all undoubtedly come from the final match against Scotland, at Murrayfield. England had not won a Grand Slam for 23 years and from the time of our opening match – when we fought back against Ireland to beat them 24–9 – everything had been building towards this terrific climax.

If I cast back now over the Scotland game, some of the most familiar memories seem almost trivial and unrepresentative; but the memories of someone who was there on the field will very likely *not* be the same as someone who was in the crowd or who watched it on television. For them the highlights will tend to be the points-scoring moments, whereas for us on the field there was a hell of a lot else going on.

In the dressing-room before the game our coach, Mike Davis, said:

'Look, lads, you only get one opportunity in your career to do this. Don't let it slip out of your grasp.'

How right he was. Up till that season the England I played for were more likely to win the wooden spoon than anything else. Now we had to face up to the possibility that we might achieve something really great – provided we kept our nerve. The fears I felt, before going out on the pitch, are an episode in themselves. As someone said about the lion and the antelope when they met face to face, both were quivering with fear – the antelope because it feared for its life, the lion from anticipation because it couldn't wait to get on with the job; any waiting about was liable to produce doubts in the lion's mind that something might go wrong and allow the antelope to escape. For us the similar fear, of being unsuccessful after all the work we had put in, was almost unbearable.

One thing that eased the tension was a running joke I had with Andy Irvine, Scotland's captain. It started when we were on tour in New Zealand and had to deal with the extreme boredom of Sunday afternoons over there. We switched on the television to watch the wrestling, and one of the guys said to his opponent before they fought: 'The loser must leave the country.' That went down well with us – it was about as convincing as a Western with sheep – and at Murrayfield, when we tossed up before the match, Andy brought out the line again, and I remember my relief at having something to smile at.

On the field, I can remember a lot of what happened without any difficulty. The tries, for instance. I remember Clive Woodward putting Mike Slemen in. John Carleton scored three, which was quite outstanding. I also remember the Scots scoring. John Rutherford scored a great try near the end, and the way Andy Irvine was running the ball at us from any position on the field in the second half – that is something I will also never forget.

I never wanted a final whistle to go so much in all my life. We were two scores ahead, but for an awful long time the hands of the clock just weren't going round so far as I was concerned.

Afterwards, Peter Wheeler and Fran Cotton carried me off the pitch on their shoulders. Before that, Peter Wheeler came up and hugged me, and someone said I gave him a kiss. I *don't* remember that! Seriously, though, can you imagine me kissing Wheelbrace at any time, let alone while he's wearing his gumshield?

LEEKS RAMPANT

One of the better side-effects of our win in 1980 was that it made Max Boyce rewrite his material for a whole year. Twelve months earlier he had been laughing in our faces as loudly as ever. I know. I was captain of England when we suffered our highest-ever defeat in Cardiff. Maybe that's why I remember it so well. Some memories insist on screening themselves in your head even though they give you about as much pleasure as being mugged on a wet night in Tiger Bay.

We went down 27–3 and were pretty lucky to get the three. I remember only too well, as the game drifted into injury time and they were taking the final conversion, leaning against one of the posts and gasping for air. Sixty thousand Welshmen had been singing their heads off all afternoon and I thought to myself: 'Well, Bill, you've made somebody happy today'.

At times like that you want nothing more than a fast coach waiting

outside the ground to speed you back across the Severn Bridge. That, of course, is the last thing you can actually have. Instead you grin and bear it, go to the press conference and agree with all and sundry that you were murdered by a better team, then go to the dinner and repeat the dose. At least, by then, you can allow yourself a glass or two of something more palatable.

THE PESOS MILLIONAIRE

In 1981 England were the first national side to tour Argentina. No matter what happened soon afterwards between our two countries, that tour counts as one of my outstanding memories.

The Argentinians were very hospitable and we played two Tests there. We drew the first 18–18 and won the second 12–6, which was a considerable achievement for at least two reasons. Firstly, they are a strong rugby country and would certainly do well in a European competition. Secondly, we had to play our matches with a below-strength side; we played very well, and we came home unbeaten. I might add that when Argentinian supporters bay for your blood, they do it even more convincingly than the Welsh!

The only problem we encountered was the economy. Inflation was running at about 400 per cent and they devalued twice while we were there. I spent half my time trying to change my Argentinian pesos into American dollars; unfortunately, two million other people were trying to do the same as I was. Things were so crazy, I became a pesos millionaire at the races – and bankrupted myself getting a five-mile taxi ride back to the hotel.

That'll be
1,000,000 pe
seño
1,100,000...
1,200,000...
1,300,000...

HANGING FROM THE TREES

One of the greatest wins by a British side was the North's defeat of the All Blacks at Otley in 1979. In drizzly, horrible West Riding weather we beat them 21–9, scoring four tries to their one. It was a fantastic occasion for the North, and for provincial rugby everywhere; we had spectators hanging from the trees and we did them proud. To beat New Zealand, and to beat them well, as we did, is a feat that people present will not forget, especially these fifteen fellers: K.A. O'Brien; J.Carleton, A.M. Bond, A. Wright, M.A.C. Slemen; A.G.B. Old, S.J. Smith; C. White, A. Simpson, F.E. Cotton, W.B. Beaumont, J.P. Sydall, R.M. Uttley, P.J. Dixon, A. Neary.

MOVING UP TO THE THIRDS

When I was seventeen, I was a regular member of Fylde 6th XV, for whom I turned out at full-back because in those days I sensed that the glamour positions were in the backs, and a bit of glamour was what I fancied. One week, the 3rd and 1st XVs had fixtures in Newcastle at Percy Park. It was Bonfire Night, and a lot of the guys who might have gone didn't want to, so I was picked to play in the forwards for the 3rd XV.

Off I went to Newcastle. With me I took £1, which represented one-third of my weekly pocket money (I was going to the Tech. at Salford at the time, so was not exactly wealthy). We set off in the coach at nine in the morning, got to Newcastle and played the game. Everything so far had gone according to plan, and I was enjoying myself. My mother had wanted to know how long I would be away, so I'd planned it all out in advance.

'The game will finish at half-past four,' I'd told her. 'Let's say we leave at seven o'clock. So I'll be back about midnight.'

I wasn't. She went to bed but couldn't sleep. I rang from Scotch

Corner at half-past two in the morning and managed to say: 'I'm going to be a little late'. I put the phone down. (Scotch Corner, for anyone who doesn't know, is not all that far from Newcastle.)

My father had played rugby himself and spent the evening reassuring my mother that I was old enough and would certainly be all right. Now she turned to him and very firmly said: 'Right. That's it. He's never playing another game of rugby in his life!'

All that night the old stagers of the 3rd XV chipped in to buy me beer and look after me. My pound hadn't gone very far. I got home at half-past six.

The trip to Percy Park was something I am unlikely to forget. It was no great shakes from the playing point of view, but it gave me my first real insight into what the game of rugby was about.

You....will...not...play...rugby...again

AWAY DAYS – AND NIGHTS

Every boy who has played for his school knows that some away fixtures are better than others – and for reasons that have little or nothing to do with rugby. It may be the length of the coach journey which attracts, and the fact that you have to leave your school in the middle of the morning and miss a few lessons. There's also the journey back, and the fact that old So-and-so usually lets you stop off in the town of X for twenty minutes (that's two fags and a pint if you're nippy).

Or it may be because they, the other school, do a good tea. I was always extremely impressed with the tea at Rossall, a school near Fleetwood, because they had chips. At our school we never saw a chip in our lives. I remember I was so surprised, I told my mother: 'It's a great school, that,' I said to her. 'Oh, is it?' she said. 'Why?' 'You get chips afterwards.' 'Oh,' she said, and nodded in the vague way mothers do when they don't quite understand what you're on about.

I mentioned in the previous chapter the story of my first proper outing, to Newcastle. The two clubs concerned, Fylde and Gosforth, have always had a special affinity. Whenever they came down to us, we put on a disco and dance for them and they would stay till about midnight and then go home by coach. Naturally, they looked after us when we went up there, so Gosforth was always reckoned to be a good night out. Harrogate was another fixture we looked forward to because they did a good tea – and afterwards we had a favourite pub we stopped at, the Cross Keys just outside Skipton.

Generally speaking, the best away fixtures were the ones we called 'stoppers'. The decisive factor, usually, was whether the bus journey was more than four hours. If it was, we stopped, on the principle that it was better to have a good time followed by a bad journey than no good time at all, which is what you would end up with if you spent the whole of opening time on the road. Arriving home early and thirsty was never our definition of a satisfactory night-out.

Gosforth, needless to say, was a stopper; so were Leicester, Moseley, Gloucester, and anywhere in South Wales. When I played for Lancashire we usually stopped. London, too, was a stopper, but we'll come to that later.

'THE NURSES ARE COMING'

The ideal night-out would start off with a good soak in hot clean water in a big bath. To non-rugby players that may not sound all that special, but I can assure them that the average player doesn't get many of those in a season. Someone else always seems to get in there first, and you have to take your bath in a tepid sea of scum which you can't see through and which has dark bits floating in it (you don't know what these dark bits are, except that they're not yours).

After you've had this de-luxe bath you go along to the bar, meet your mates and down a few ales. Some people would have it that you go in for tea first of all, and drink the beer later. This is not the best order of play. The best order of play is: beer first, then tea, then more beer. After tea, there is often a lull in the proceedings, and you just drink slowly until eight o'clock or so. If there's going to be a dance it will start about then, at which point you accelerate the drinking and keep right on until the end of the party.

Some clubs take their rugby more seriously nowadays, and have tended to neglect the entertainment side of things. I myself think this is a shame, but there you are; most people remain faithful to their own background, and when I started playing rugby we rated the evenings as an important part of the fixture.

Even in those days you couldn't take it for granted that your hosts would lay something on for you, but over the years players could get a pretty shrewd idea of what was likely to happen. Opposing teams used to chat to each other more than they do now, and in cases of doubt the captain could always ask: 'Anything on tonight?' 'Oh, yeah.

We've got a do laid on'. Back to the lads. 'Right. They've fixed this do for us. So we're stopping'.

One or two of the guys were so keen on the disco-ing, etcetera, that they travelled to the match in jeans and a sweater, and kept the fancy dancing gear beside them on a coat hanger. They must have been bachelors, that's all I can think, and didn't like the idea of losing out to the home team if any spare birds were going. Not that there ever were many. If you asked your hosts about this, the standard reply was: 'It's all fixed. We've rung the nurses' home'. 'Oh, great'.

For me the big attraction of these nights was the cameraderie with the rest of the lads – the chat, the laughs, the beer, and no more worries till Monday. Around midnight, the ideal night-out would move into its final phase as we boarded the bus and set sail for home. I used to take a sleeping bag and a pillow with me, and when I had risen to be a senior member of the side I used to stretch out across the back seat and grab some sleep. A couple of hours into the journey it was always appreciated if we could stop at a cafe for a really good grease-up. By then we'd be starving, having put nothing into our stomachs except beer since the tea. Then on we'd roll, and the next thing many of us knew, we were being dropped somewhere in the general vicinity of our homes. It's surprising how quickly you sober up if you have to do the last mile to your door on foot when it's several hours before dawn on a freezing Sunday morning.

As for any other stops we might make on the way, these were very much at the discretion of the driver – and we all know that coach drivers hate stopping. On my very first big journey home I learned that the organized pee-stop is a rarity. With that particular driver the answer was to prise up one of the floorboards above the drive-shaft, and perform through the gap. Other drivers, if you were nice to them, would let you open the door and do it into the morning breeze – not forgetting to hold tightly to the rail with the other hand. Other arrangements were made from time to time, all of them too primitive

to discuss here. Nowadays, of course, posh coaches have toilets.

One of the most understanding drivers I ever met took us to a match about three or four hours from home. There was some doubt among the players after the match over whether we should stop or head for home. The driver gave himself the casting vote. 'We're bloody stopping,' he said. 'I like it here.'

THE LONDON TRIP

If we had a fixture in London we used to take the train and stay down there, although we usually left the club itself at around seven-thirty. This was because the host team used to push off then to drive to wherever they lived; unlike Fylde, where nearly all the members were locals, the lads who played for London clubs might have to commute quite a distance to the ground. It was no great hardship to us – we'd find a pub in the centre of Town somewhere and catch the night sleeper home.

The club wouldn't pay for a sleeper, but I reckoned a second-class sleeper ticket was very reasonable and well worth the outlay, so I used to get one and pack a bunch of the lads in there, all well kitted out with plenty of cans to see us through the journey. The train used to reach Preston at about three-thirty and pull into a siding. You could either get off then or stay on board till about seven. In the morning there would be a succession of bleary figures leaving the train and picking their way across the tracks, exchanging the smoky railway compartment which must have stunk like a brewery – or worse – for a couple of hours' sleep at home followed, ideally, by a big Sunday morning fry-up.

Looking for a night sleeper, boys?...

Those away days gave me some of the most enjoyable times of my life. Players who have done similar trips will know what I mean, and to me the recipe is very simple – you go off for a few hours with a bunch of like-minded fellers, you have a few drinks, share a few laughs, jokes, maybe a song or two, and then you come home again, nicely warmed by the booze and the camaraderie, and look forward to the next trip.

Try telling that to a woman, however, and you find they do not understand what you are talking about. Hilary, my wife, has been very sympathetic over the years, and I should not like anyone to think I am picking on her. As it happens, I don't have to, because it is a bewildering fact that 99 per cent of wives and girlfriends of rugby players cannot for the life of them see what pleasure we get from these outings and the fact that we enjoy our own company so much. A woman will say, when her husband eventually comes in, some time before breakfast, and slumps down in his favourite chair and starts beaming at the wallpaper: 'But you lost. I heard it on the radio. You lost 42–10. What are you looking so pleased about?'

The husband shakes his head slowly, a stupid sentimental grin all over his face. 'Never mind the game,' he says. 'It was a bloody good night out.'

Now the wife shakes her head. 'Men,' she says. 'You do it deliberately.'

Of course we do.

MY MOST MEMORABLE TRIES

This is going to be a short chapter because try-scoring was not my forte. In fact we considered just putting the title at the top of this page and leaving the rest of it blank. But then I thought, no, I *have* scored a few, even if the great majority were not at the highest level, and if I can describe some of them it might help the morale of a few props and second-row forwards out there who have yet to experience the thrill of personally scoring four points all in one go.

I never scored a try for England, but I have been very close. Once, against Ireland, I was stopped a yard from the line. Well, not exactly stopped, more half-stopped; enough – as I thought – to make me turn and pass the ball back. If I had kept on going, I would have scored. I can be sure of that because the guy who tackled me was Colin Patterson, the Irish scrum-half, who was about five feet four and the smallest player on the field. Afterwards the lads said: 'Why didn't you go through?' and I didn't have much of an answer for them.

Let no-one think, however, that I have not had my moments. W.B. Beaumont has scored tries on tour for the Lions in provincial games, and he also scored in the Welsh Centenary match when England-Wales played Scotland-Ireland. In that match I received the ball one yard out and, being deadly at that kind of distance, never lost my pace and went clean over. The combined power of two nations could not keep me out. A great moment. At the dinner I heard someone describing my try: 'He got the ball about two feet out and sort of fell over.' Very charitable. Some people have no sense of magic.

I also have perfect recall of the moment in an England trial game when I intercepted John Horton's pass on the half-way line. This put me clean through but when I looked up it was all too clear that I still had fifty yards to cover. I thought: 'Bloody hell, this is going to have to be a team effort.' So I gave the ball to Maurice Colclough. He carried it for a bit and passed it on, and eventually one of our lads scored. Afterwards someone said: 'Why did you give it to Maurice? He was going even slower than you were.'

One thing I have learned about this try-scoring lark: as soon as you come out of the pack and do something really distinctive where everyone can see you, all you get for it is a load of criticism. It takes me back to the moment I mentioned earlier, when I first discovered at school that forwards were allowed to score. I might have been better off if they had left me in ignorance. All right, I know there's nothing in the rules barring forwards from scoring and I was bound to find out one day if I kept playing long enough. But I can't help feeling that not everyone is glad when a forward does score. I'm sure some of the backs don't like it, for instance, especially if it happens more than once in a game because it makes them look redundant as well as hurting their feelings. I just wonder if it goes any further.

Take kicking. I used to fancy myself as a goal-kicker when I was at school. But as soon as I got to senior rugby at Fylde they said: 'No way.' The reasons they gave made sense at the time. 'We can't have a forward dragging himself up from a scrum and then, while he's still blowing like an old cart-horse, expect him to kick goals from all angles.' They wanted someone who'd be a bit more composed, they said, someone with a bit of energy left who could concentrate properly on what he had to do to get the ball over the bar.

At the time I went along with it. Only now am I beginning to wonder why it is that forwards get so few of the star parts. I would be curious to know if any forwards reading this book have ever had similar doubts. I mean, why should anyone want to keep us out of the limelight? It can't have anything to do with the way we look. Can it?

If Rip van Winkle was a rugby player, and woke up from his deep sleep after twenty years to find that someone had put a ticket in his pocket for next Saturday's international, I wonder if he'd understand what was going on when he got to the match.

The metric business is something Rip might dimly remember because it was being talked about shortly before he went to sleep. All the same, I bet he still thinks imperial – like the rest of us – and is relieved to find that the old boy who marks out the pitch at his local club is using exactly the same measurements as he always used to.

Mind you, what with the way Paul Thorburn has been putting over kicks lately from sixty and sixty-five yards, rugby pitches ought to be getting larger, not staying the same. Last time out for Rip van Winkle, there wasn't much danger of someone kicking a goal from fifty or even forty yards, especially in the second half when the old soggy ball was in its prime and a ten-yard kick was reckoned good going. (With the toe, of course. None of that poncy soccer-style round-the-corner stuff.)

Those old rugby balls were one of the wonders of a bygone age. Some of them were more round than oval to look at, they had as much bounce in them as an old grapefruit, and with a quarter of an hour to go on a wet afternoon in February they were as much of a joy to handle as a medicine ball in the gym.

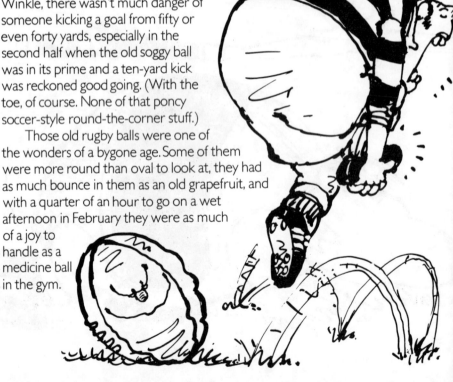

BOUNCING BOMBS

Another big change has been to the touch-kicking law. Never mind what Rip van Winkle thinks, I am sure this is a change for the better because it has forced players to think more about attacking and has also done the spectators a big favour by ending those terrible boring spectacles where the scrum-half used to do nothing but work the line, pushing his forwards upfield five yards at a time. Nowadays some players are so good at kicking to touch and making the ball bounce before it goes out that they have almost got round this change in the law, but there is one important difference. Now when they do it they are usually attacking, and the kick is the last part of a move aimed at putting the forwards well inside the opposition's twenty-two. So the touch-kick is used to create a real scoring opportunity, not as a way of loitering anxiously in midfield and getting nowhere.

One of the best exponents of the bouncing kick was Gareth Edwards. He had it worked out so well that it seemed he could thread the ball at will through the opposition and send it bouncing or rolling into touch at just the right point to demoralize the other side and make his own forwards scent that a score was on if they could win the line-out. Unlike most other kickers, whose efforts sometimes land badly and skid sideways, or stand up on end, Gareth's kicks always followed a true, low course, the ball travelling end-on like a dambuster's bomb.

While I suspect that Gareth would agree with much that I have to say about changes in the law, I must confess I was puzzled the other day when during an international he said on television that he would like to see a ban put on wheeling the scrum because it spoiled the pattern of play. I couldn't understand it at first because I can't see anything wrong with wheeling. To me it's all part of the game. Then I realized what it was all about. He wasn't criticizing the wheel as such, what he was really saying was that as a member of the scrum-halves' union he didn't like it because it made things untidy for him. I've heard that kind of talk before: it's like Steve Smith and scrummaging practice. He used to hate doing it because, as he said, his hands got so cold. He was the same at line-outs. If the ball came down a yard or two from where he had positioned himself and he had to bend down, he used to complain. 'Come on, lads,' he'd say. 'Give it straight to me. I don't want to have to stretch about all over the place.'

A PASS FOR MR. STEVE SMITH!

In Praise Of Grovelling

Unlike twenty years ago, when it took years of argument and discussion before one of the laws was changed, today there is something new every season. If you take the rules about rucking and mauling, they are now very different from what they were even when I was playing. A short while back, you could grovel on the ground, pick the ball out and hand it back to somebody; now you would be penalized for doing it. Personally I can't see any real need to change the system – and not just because it was one of my specialities. Grovelling was at least constructive; the player was trying to play the ball. And while I am against people killing the ball, I think referees are coming in too fast and blowing up even when the ball is on the point of leaving the ruck. I would like to see the law being modified in such a way that referees allow a certain amount of grovelling provided the ball is being fairly contested; play is then kept on the move and there isn't that continual resort to set-pieces.

Where safety is an important consideration, I am in favour of changing the law – as when the flying wedge was banned because it was too dangerous for schoolboy players. Nowadays, too, the minimum height of the scrum is controlled by law to prevent ambitious hookers from getting so low they could nod the ball back with their head. I don't think that's very clever, at least not in the medium to long term (even hookers' heads weren't designed for kicking practice) and so I approve of the law which now states that in a scrum a player's shoulders may not be lower than his hips. It may not get rid of collapsing scrums but it must help.

Life in the scrum is grim enough without the undignified business of collapsing, which is really another word for having your nose rammed into the ground or into whatever was immediately in front of it before the moment of collapse. If you're in the second row, I can tell you, you're in a really nice position. You're in the dark, bound to your partner with one arm while the other arm is somewhere between the legs of the prop in front of you. When your pack is going forwards you hang on to the waistband of his shorts; when it's going backwards you have to give him a bit of encouragement. People think what a glamorous role you play in there, at the heart of things, in what they usually insist on calling the 'engine room'. They should try pushing for eighty minutes behind Fran Cotton or Phil Blakeway.

GOING UP!

Line-outs have been tidied up a lot in the last few years, mainly I suspect for the benefit of referees. In the old days of the double-banked line, with every player breathing down a teammate's neck and those in the line standing within a comfortable elbow's reach of the opposition, much of the evil goings-on could be concealed from the officials' view.

Now that the two lines are spaced out so much and referees can insist on there being such a big gap between the two sides, it looks as though some of the old skills could be lost to the game. I'm thinking for instance of the ancient art of lifting, combined with the other very difficult task of hanging in space for up to twenty seconds in such a way that the referee thinks you are doing it entirely under your own steam.

If skills like that were removed from the game of rugby, we might as well take up basketball.

Look, ref, we're not playing until we hear it talk

Players are bigger than they used to be. The difference in size between the second-row forwards of the Sixties and those of the Eighties is far greater than many people may remember. The French, in particular, have always managed to produce the occasional giant, but by 1976 they were showing signs of going into mass-production.

Although Wales won the Championship that year the French had the best side. I remember going over to play them at Parc des Princes. We thought we had a good-sized pack of forwards, but theirs were *massive*. They had Gerard Cholley, who was the French Army heavyweight boxing champion; a guy called Bastiat, who looked at least eight feet tall; Imbernon, a giant second-row; and Michel Palmié, also enormous. All of them wore about three days' growth of beard and were dead-menacing.

I stood there waiting for the kick-off. The partisan atmosphere in that stadium was tremendous – if you're French. The Dax band was thumping away, fireworks were shooting up in the air, thousands of well-oiled Frenchmen were roaring their heads off. I thought: 'What on earth am I doing here?' and offered a silent prayer. Twenty yards away, Palmié must have been doing the same thing because I saw him cross himself just before the kick-off. At the end of the game, after we'd been beaten by 30 points to 9, I thought: 'Well, He must have been listening to Palmié, not Beaumont.'

No other country creates the Romans v Christians atmosphere quite like the French, and no visiting player can run out on to the Parc des Princes without feeling he is one of the sacrificial victims being served up for that afternoon's entertainment. At the best of times the English have a tendency to regard foreign, i.e. overseas, opposition as somehow superhuman and therefore invincible. I sometimes wonder if the French haven't worked this out for themselves, and are using it for their own benefit.

I certainly had qualms the first couple of times I played against them. In those days their game was dominated by massive packs, and the moment of truth tended to arrive early in the game. This was just as well because the only way to play against guys like that is to get stuck into them. If you don't, two things will happen: they will flatten you, and then add insult to injury (literally) by releasing their backs to run rings round your side for the rest of the game.

I remember playing in Perpignan one day in November (they might have told them it was Armistice Day). We went out there on Sunday to play the match on Tuesday. That meant we'd been on the wine for just about three days before we got on the field. In the first minute of the game we won a penalty, which is a pretty rare happening in France so we decided to take a kick at goal. Our kicker managed to land it on their twenty-two. One of the French team caught it – and they were off. Four or five scissors movements later (it hurt your eyes if you tried to count them all) they were touching down underneath our posts. They took the kick, no trouble, and about a minute and a half into the game we were 6–0 down. I turned to a pal of mine called Nick Trickey, who was playing in the second row.

I said: 'Look. This could be slightly embarrassing.'

He agreed with me. He said: 'Yes, it could.'

Fortunately, we weren't so far gone that we couldn't stage a recovery, and in the end, despite having a gallon of wine on board per man, we lost only narrowly. Eighty minutes earlier, I wouldn't have counted on it. There is something threatening about French backs on the move which is in almost complete contrast with the heavy artillery tactics of the forwards. They somehow manage to *look* faster than our lot. They are *chic* in appearance and wear those little shorts with the vee in the sides, and my wife has been known to comment favourably on their 'nice brown legs' – although I cannot see what real bearing any of that flash stuff has on the speed with which they cover the ground. The answer, maybe, is in the nature of the ground itself. The French play a game which is tailor-made for the hard, fast pitches of Southern France where most of their best players come from.

If you watch them work a passing movement, they are extremely ingenious in their control and variation of pace. The guy with the ball does not necessarily run at full speed, but then he passes it to someone who bursts into the line at a hundred miles an hour, catches the opposition unawares and goes through them before they can adjust to the variation. Even if he doesn't quite get through, he can still pass the ball outside, and his burst may have done enough to disrupt the defensive cover which suddenly finds it has left their winger with that fatal extra yard; he needs no further invitation and nips over in the corner; quatre points, as they say.

A Great Fixture

Although a stretch of water separates the Irish from the other Home Nations, I wouldn't go so far as to describe them as foreigners. Different, yes, but not as different as the French. Just as there is a family relationship between Guinness drinkers and bitter men, in Dublin you can always feel you're on something quite like home territory (whereas in Paris if your hosts have been ladling a mixture of Pernod and wine into you for several hours you can't always be sure where you are).

Lansdowne Road is always a great fixture. The Irish are glad to see you, they give you a warm welcome followed by a hard game, and afterwards you get stuck into the black stuff with never a trace of bad feeling. The Irish, it seems, know how to keep things in proportion: if they win, they don't gloat, and if they lose they don't complain.

Playing against the Irish in Dublin can be daunting. When you look at the crowd you see a horde of ruddy faces who have gathered from all over the country – from Cork, Limerick, Belfast, everywhere – for a great and wonderful hooley which they hope will include giving the English a good bashing on the field. Their players respond to this by tearing about the place for eighty minutes like demented flies, filling the visitor with the uneasy conviction that there must be at least thirty green shirts in action.

Dublin is always special to me because I made my début there – called in on the Friday when Roger Uttley had to drop out. I was twenty-two. My opposite number in the line-out was a man for whom I had – and still have – enormous respect, Willie-John McBride, one of the great international captains. As we lined up together for the first time I said to myself: 'Bill, whatever you do, don't upset him.'

I was true to my word. Willie-John had what must have been the easiest game of his life. As for me, I was just happy to survive to fight another day. Fortunately my lack of aggression in the line-out must have been put down to inexperience and I was forgiven.

I was not always so discreet against the Irish. When Phil Blakeway went off injured I had to prop against Phil Orr. After the first scrum I made the mistake of saying, with foolish bravado: 'Is that the best you can do, Phil?' He proceeded to show me in no uncertain terms that he was capable of very much more. After a bit, Peter Wheeler said to me: 'Why don't you keep your gob shut!'

Willie Duggan was another tough individual. To some extent – if you ignore his size – he was a very unlikely-looking rugby player. He had a totally white face, and he used to chain-smoke right up to the start of a game. Then he'd go out there and play like a man possessed. In New Zealand he was regularly kicked to pieces but never complained; his answer to the opposition's hard guys was to get up and do it all again. As a team man he was invaluable.

Is that the best you can do, Phil?.... Ha Ha Ha...Is that the best you can do, Phil?Ho Ho... Is that the best you can do, Phil?.... Hee Hee..Is that....

CATCHING SPRINGBOKS

Man for man, the South Africans seemed always to be that bit larger than us. Six feet eight, six feet nine, they were a breed apart. At first I couldn't see how on earth we were going to get the ball, then Fran Cotton and I formed this plan whereby he stood on the feller's toes while I went for the ball. We called it 'legalized lifting'; it helped us to get by.

When you socialize with them, you find that these Afrikaners aren't as grim as they look. Their hospitality is good, and they are really quite a friendly bunch of fellers. Not warm like the Irish, they must

39

have been hewn from a harder type of rock, but you can have a friendly understanding with them just as you can with rugby players the world over. You notice slight differences, of course. After the match, for instance, when 'Moaner' Van Heerden wants to commiserate or congratulate, he comes over and shakes your hand and then he pulls your head towards his and cracks them together – in the friendliest possible way. It's just his method of saying 'Thanks for the game.' After a while you get used to this sort of thing. At first your eyes may spin round like strawberries in a fruit machine, but then you accept it as part of the way they do things over there.

PUNCHING WALLABIES

Our tour to Australia in 1975 must have been one of the roughest on record. They kicked off in the Brisbane Test and steamed straight into us with boots flying. There wasn't a pretence of playing rugby. We then had a line-out. Both sets of forwards joined in a huge fight; I got punched and went off the field for six stitches in my eye.

After three minutes Mike Burton was sent off for a late tackle. I was already in the dressing-room when he arrived, getting my faced fixed up so I could go back on the field.

I said to him: 'What's up with you?'

He didn't say a word. It wasn't until I had been patched up and was halfway back to the pitch I suddenly realized he had been sent off. Alec Lewis, our manager, confirmed this, then asked me if I'd ever played prop before.

'No,' I said.

'Well, here's your chance to find out,' was his reply.

There hadn't been a scrum before I was back on the field, so I ended up propping in every scrum of the game. We only lost one scrum against our put-in all afternoon, so I wasn't displeased with my performance, unplanned though it had been.

Meanwhile back in the dressing-room, Fran Cotton had arrived to console Mike Burton who was now realizing that he had a new reputation to live with – the first man to be sent off while wearing an England jersey.

'Hell,' said Mike, 'fancy being sent off for a late tackle.'

'Well,' said Fran, 'it can't have been all that late. You'd only been playing for three minutes.'

Fortunately, for us and for the game, the next Australians we met were a very different bunch of lads and we got on very well with them. I became good friends with Andy Slack, their captain, and if ever I'm over there on business I look him up and we have a couple of jars together. Peace has been restored, and we hope our successors can ensure that it stays that way.

CHASING KIWIS

Even when he's carrying a sheep under each arm, a New Zealand international is not an easy man to keep up with. Year in and year out they play rugby to a standard that makes them the best in the world.

But, when it comes down to it, rugby players are the same kind of guys whichever country they play for. Every time I have toured abroad I have been made welcome. I've collected a few bruises, and I haven't always enjoyed the results of our matches, but the entertainment and the company after the game have never failed to give me good memories.

JAPANESE DO IT UPSIDE DOWN

Even the Japanese were not all that different. Admittedly, they have evolved some strange techniques to make up for their lack of height against Western opposition. At a line-out, their hooker threw to the feet of the prop. The prop was obviously expecting this because he jumped up in the air and let the ball pass underneath him. Then my opponent at No 2 dived towards the ground and caught the ball. All the while I was standing there waiting for a normal ball over the top.

I thought to myself: 'I'd better put a stop to this.'

At the second line-out I was ready. The ball came in low and true; the Japanese prop jumped over it and my opponent was halfway to the floor when I stuck out a boot and struck the ball cleanly away. It was a brilliant interception, the ball flew straight to their fly-half who immediately tried to drop a goal.

I thought to myself: 'Forget it! Let them have as much ball as they want.'

They had some other line-out variations which I thought were pretty cunning. Four guys would shoot up in the air, and take our guys with them; but they were decoys. Then the real catcher would rise and the ball would go straight to him. To get away with a ploy like that you need really good timing; the Japanese had plenty of that, in fact they had obviously dissected that aspect of the game with enormous care to try and see what they could possibly do to win the ball against taller rivals who were trained jumpers and could be expected to dominate the air. The answers they came up with relied instead on surprise and immaculate timing, and served them very well.

We only beat the Japanese by a couple of points when we played there, so they must have come on at a remarkable rate in the last few years – like so many other nations in the Pacific area. If you look, for instance, at the results of the 1985 Hong Kong Sevens you find that Western Samoa not only reached the semi-finals, they were 8–0 up against Australia at half-time before going out 16–8. Several other 'surprise' sides distinguished themselves, and I can tell you a little more about two of them.

FRIENDLY ISLANDS

The national stadium of Tonga left a little bit to be desired when we arrived there. We had to find a brick to smash the padlock off the changing-room door so we could have somewhere to put our boots on (we had come ready-changed from the hotel).

The pitch was full of rocks, and holes where rocks had been, so we asked our hosts to remove the rocks and fill the holes. They brought up some coral sand and used that for a filler. I can't think of anything sharper or more abrasive to land on outside of broken glass, and very quickly the play became concentrated on those parts of the field which had no coral sand traps. I felt in a way fortunate not to be playing. I was injured at the time, but I made it my business to see that most of the rocks were off the field before play began.

Tonga was fascinating, but much more primitive than I had imagined. The only piece of tarmac on the island was the airstrip; the roads were dirt tracks through the jungle. The hotel where we stayed had a very grand-sounding name which I have forgotten; nothing worked in the entire place, and the dominant feature was its atmosphere of quiet disintegration. We were invited to a special banquet where the main treat was to eat chunks of local pig which had been wrapped in leaves and cooked in an earth pit. Some of the lads were doubling up on their Alka-Seltzer rations that night.

Of course, it was very generous of our hosts to lay on the banquet. I seem to remember we tried to repay them by donating a pig. When you come from Europe, it's easy to forget how radically different the standard of living may be on a remote Pacific island. These Tongans certainly didn't have much in reserve. If you offered your cigarette packet to someone, twenty hands reached out.

On the rugby field, they played a loose running game, throwing the ball around all over the place. They were good, but our lads were able to handle them (we were confident also in the powers of the referee that we had brought with us) and there were no shock results.

Unlike in Fiji. When I went there with the Lions in 1977 they beat us. We were, it has to be said, very tired at the end of our tour, but their kind of dashing, aggressive rugby did take us by surprise. So did some of the decisions of the Fijian referee. We didn't mind the three penalties he awarded our way, it was the twenty-odd he gave them…

Physically, the Fijians are very impressive. Magnificent athletes with enormous legs on them – that is how they first appear to any visiting team. The visitor then learns to get his tackles in quick, because once those fellers get moving, their knees coming up above their heads, it's like trying to stop a tank with your bare hands.

Added to these physical problems is another factor which cannot be ignored: the weather. I've been in Fiji a couple of times and the last time we played there it was 100°F with about 80 per cent humidity. As you stepped into the open the heat just fell round you like a blanket.

I thought to myself: 'Whatever we do, we mustn't let them have any ball at all, otherwise we'll be totally knackered after ten minutes.'

On this second occasion I was with the England team and we managed to score enough points and keep them out sufficiently to get our win. Looking back, I think we scraped home on merit, but I also recall a conversation I had before the match with a loyal Fijian subject. Reminding me that we would be playing on the Queen's birthday, he said:

'Of course, we'd like to win, but really we think the Queen would be unhappy if we beat you on her birthday.'

I thought to myself: 'What a lovely feller. We could do with a few more opponents like you!'

ANATOMY OF A VET

As opposed to the gentleman who spends half his nights buried beneath the odorous flanks of pregnant farm animals, the rugby vet enjoys a softer life. The nearest he gets to the farmyard scenario is when he packs down for the occasional scrum, but in his case scrums are seen not so much as places of work as somewhere for chaps to lean against other chaps and grab a bit of a rest.

Veterans' rugby has evolved as a graceful offshoot from the main body of club rugby. In status it is roughly level with the 5th or 6th XV in the average provincial club, but in nature it is very different from the all-running, jumping and tackling game pursued by the younger members.

At its best (or least physically taxing) veterans' rugby is a slow possession game in which the team with the ball moves methodically up the field passing the ball to each other in a series of rationed moves. No-one is expected to carry the ball more than five or ten yards, and there is a tacit understanding with the opposition that you never tackle a man in possession provided he stays in the bunch and doesn't run very fast. The only effective counter to this kind of massed passing move it to hold a few of your fattest men in reserve and at the appropriate time bring them forward to steamroller the other side and bring play, ideally, to a complete stop.

In more than one way, the veterans' game is like the under-tens' rugby we met in the first chapter. Most of the players involved mill up and down the pitch in a large clump. Tackling is minimal – and in the case of Stan, our blind-side flanker in the mauve shorts, it is expressly forbidden on grounds of age; Stan claims to be over seventy.

The pattern with kicking is similar too, but for different reasons. In boys' rugby, tactical kicking would be acceptable if anyone could do it properly; in practice it is rarely seen. The vets, for their part, don't like it because although one or two of the lads can do a reasonable up-

and-under, it means an awful lot of chasing. Experience has shown, moreover, that any ball kicked more than twenty yards ahead of the attacking side, regardless of how high in the air it goes, is bound to land among the opposition giving them plenty of time to start a counter-move. In their defence, some habitual kickers reckon that up-and-unders are worthwhile if more than fifty per cent produce a knock-on; but this is a minority view. Through-kicks to the corner-flag or thereabouts are also frowned on because they so seldom come off, leaving the rest of the team to chase forwards and backwards in a quite unnecessary manner. It is sometimes necessary to remind vet scrum-halves that they never were as good as Gareth Edwards in the first place, let alone at twice his age.

TRAINING FOR VETS

Most dedicated rugby vets are careful to observe three basic laws relating to body maintenance. These are:
1. Their bodies are wearing out. Not all the bits are wearing out at the same rate, but they must be prepared to expect diminished performance in the future.
2. They should reschedule downwards their physical aims in life.
3. The best way to be match-fit within the limits of this new schedule is to attend weekly training.

Training is important to rugby vets, in fact they talk about it more than any other type of club player from the 1st XV down to the Colts. If you have ever worked in the same office as a rugby vet you will know what I mean.

Clients and fellow-workers learn that there are few questions that a rugby vet cannot deflect into the path of his prowess at rugby, or, rather, his prowess at training for rugby. A simple remark like 'Morning, George, how are you?' is a gift. One eyebrow goes up, he rubs his hands together and sails in:

'Fine, thank you, fine.' (Pause) 'Went training last night.'

It is, by itself, a very small remark – only four words – and yet, when delivered in the discreetly modest tone that he always uses, a blend of librarian and churchwarden, it takes on a much larger character. By letting on that he has recently done something that his listener has not, and that, moreover, this something has enhanced his physical well-being whereas his listener is the same ball of flab he was two days ago, and that, moreover, this something was performed behind the exclusive doors of a club to which he belongs and his listener does not – all this does wonders for his ego, puts him in a position of superiority vis-à-vis his listener, and pre-empts any probing questions about what kind of training it really was.

With a little care and imagination, a true vet can spin out his references to the training session to fill nearly a whole week. Suitable variations on the basic 'Went training last night' are:

'Got training tonight/tomorrow/day of the week.' As in 'Sorry. Can't make it tonight/tomorrow/Thursday, etc.'

'Why not?'

'Got training.'

Or: 'Fine, thank you, fine. I'm fine *now*. Not looking foward to tonight, though.'

'Oh, why's that?'

'Got training.'

Longer timespans can also be used, such as 'the other day'. As in 'Not so bad, thank you, not *so* bad… Had a bit of a knock the other

2 laps,
5 press-ups,
8 sit-ups.....
12 pints!

day, though. (Pause) At training.'

Anyone mean enough to spy on our hero during his training nights might well come up with a different version of events. In veterans' training, for instance, the likelihood of getting even 'a bit of a knock' is very remote for the simple reason that there is no physical contact. Of course, he may trip over in the dressing-room, or fall down in the car park afterwards, but there is no question of his being tackled or anything dangerous.

What happens on vet training nights is roughly as follows. The lads arrive in ones and twos over a period of forty-five minutes to an hour and sit smoking and chatting in the dressing-room. When everyone has arrived, they put on their gear. Those wearing boots make a lot of impressive stamping noises while those with expensive Japanese trainers bounce about a bit and silently admire themselves. Then they go out to the field and jog round the outside of the pitch a few times. This is followed by a convenient number of press-ups...and it's over. Back they go, walking this time, for a nice hot bath and then it's into the clubhouse for a few pints – more, probably, than the number of laps they completed.

WHAT MAKES THEM RUN?

Veterans have done very well for themselves since they started in earnest, or 'came out', a few years back. They have filled a curious gap which previously existed between the bottom team at the club, which may well have included a few natural or 'closet' vets, and the old codgers who occupy one end of the bar and reminisce aggressively about an age far beyond anyone else's powers of recall.

Vets, in a word, are different. They play the game at their own pace, they train and drink at their own pace. Another area in which they like to be eccentric is…bathing.

Vets do not like dirty bath water. They have played enough games to feel they deserve something better than another team's leftovers. And now they are able to do it. By playing only fifteen minutes each way, they can be sure that if they start in reasonable time, and they are mercifully spared any long and embarrassing injuries, they will be first back in the clubhouse – and first in the bath! Magic.

Another advantage that vets enjoy over most other teams in the club stems from their material well-being. They have reached an age where they prefer to do things in relative comfort, and if they can

To be first in the bath brings out the only action you'll see all afternoon

afford it as well – why not? Short tours are popular with veteran sides, not so much to the traditional places but to somewhere a little bit different. Five or six days in Northern France, for instance – Thursday to Tuesday with a couple of games – that is more their mark. They will stay in quite good hotels, what is more (like their mates who go on package golf holidays to Southern Spain) and there will be champagne at half-time.

Looked at in this light, veterans' rugby makes good sense. Guys of a certain age don't want to rough it any more, they don't want to blow themselves up by running too far or to have seven bells knocked out of them by an eighteen-year-old who's on his way up and wants to be noticed – which is very much what used to happen in the XVs at the bottom of the heap, where all ages congregated. Let's have something a bit more tranquil, they decided. And now they've got it.

The average vet is very attached to his club. Even when he packs in playing at the age of fifty or so – or considerably more if he feels like it – there will still be a place for him, perhaps on the committee. Even if he does not rise quite so far, thanks either to fate or personal preference, he will usually be a keen and generous supporter of the club's activities, putting his hand in his pocket when the need arises and, one way and another, keeping in fairly close contact for the rest of his days.

Some vets have wives. In fact, quite a lot of vets have wives. And children. And they're not just kids, these children, they're large hirsute offspring with firm opinions of their own, which tend to include a strong aversion to the game of rugby.

Some of these wives occasionally wonder when the old man will stop mucking around at that club of his, or at least retire from playing before he loses every scrap of dignity. This is a forlorn question, because he has no intention of giving up his Saturday afternoons with the lads. He plans to keep going down to the club for as long as there is breath in his body. The alternative is too horrible to think about.

The alternative is to take the wife shopping!

I will declare myself here. I have every sympathy. The last thing I want to do is trail round the supermarkets on Saturday afternoon. How any self-respecting sportsman can bring himself down to that level is not something I want to know about.

I have had the offer, mind you. Once when I had a week off my wife said: 'Will you come shopping?'

I said: 'I will not! I'd rather sit here and watch *Grandstand* than go out shopping!'

So far, she hasn't asked again.

ME AND MY MONITOR

Commentating is a lot harder than some people think it is. I was quite surprised to find this out about two minutes after I started doing it for real. Up till then I had heard the guys who are now my colleagues doing it and thought it must be pretty easy. I couldn't see what the problems were. On the other hand, why didn't they spot things which to me were fairly obvious? As I was to learn, there's no place like the hot seat for finding out how it works.

The first lesson is: use your monitor. There's no point in talking about something if the viewers at home are looking at something else. In Paris for my first commentary job, it all looked a pushover. I was there with Nigel Starmer-Smith for the France-England match and thoroughly enjoying it. We were four or five storeys up in a little glass box; it was nice and warm in there while everybody else in the ground was freezing. I looked forward to a relaxed afternoon watching the game while Nigel did most of the work; I would come in occasionally with a comment.

My first chance came before the kick-off while the band was playing and the cameras were focussing on some people in the crowd. I looked down. The players were out on the pitch and I was delighted to see my old mates Phil Blakeway and Maurice Colclough. When it was my turn to speak I launched into an unhurried description of these two and what good-looking lads they were. Unfortunately the pictures on the monitor were of anything but Phil and Maurice and nobody knew what on earth I was rambling on about.

'The monitor!' hissed a voice, which I learned to recognize as that of the producer. 'Look at your monitor!'

So that was me several points down before the game had even started! Still, it's no good panicking or you'd just be piling one cock-up on top of the one before. In time you come to understand this, also that in a live broadcast you can never eradicate what has been done already.

Yes, I've had the pleasure of playing with Phil and Maurice for years and what's more they're the best of friends *off* the field.....

THE MONITOR, BILL, LOOK AT YOUR BLOODY MONITOR!

ENGLAND

England

MONITOR-2

LA WHO?

Another thing that a new commentator soon learns is that he is expected to put in a good deal of homework. This means going to watch the sides in training so you can identify players and get an idea of the moves they are likely to make in the match.

When I began doing commentary for BBC Television I had just stopped playing and so I knew virtually all the players, their styles and the positions they took up on the field. Later, of course, new players began to arrive that I'd barely heard of, let alone seen, so it was essential that I briefed myself properly at training on the Friday before the international. If I did my homework well I would then automatically know, for example, who would pick the ball up when it went out of camera shot.

One man who got away was a French winger called Lagisquet. I was over in Paris for their match against Ireland in 1984. Ollie Campbell had a kick charged down about fifteen yards from the French line. The defenders fed the ball out quickly to this winger who then ran eighty yards up the field with it.

By the time I got to talk about the incident, it was being replayed in slow motion. Eighty yards can be a very long way in slow motion when the commentator has got a fit of the mumbles because he either can't remember or can't pronounce a player's name. The producer, who was in the box, was going 'Lagisquet, Lagisquet!' to me but it was no good. The part of me which pronounces strange French names had obviously taken a short holiday.

Another thing you learn early on is to be impartial. You are broadcasting to the whole of Britain and a lot of your audience won't thank you for saying 'we' instead of 'England'. Similarly, Gareth Edwards and Bill McLaren have to be careful they don't get too enthusiastic for Wales and Scotland (respectively). It used to be even tougher for Bill when his son-in-law, Alan Lawson, was playing scrum-half for Scotland, but in fact I have only once seen him get emotional about the outcome of a match and that was when Scotland won the Grand Slam in 1984. He will not deny that he choked a little that afternoon, allowing the audience a glimpse of the private man to whom it obviously meant so much.

Since the business with Lagisquet, I like to think I have got a little bit better at the job. I have been known to confuse Roger Baird with Keith Robertson, but that was a momentary aberration and we soldier on. The main thing with player-recognition is that the commentator must do his homework so he knows what a player looks like from every angle, and can put a name to a number instantly, without thinking about it. If the player is in a blue jersey and has No. 8 on his back – it's John Beattie. If he links up in a move with 2, 3 and 5, they are Colin Deans, Ian Milne, Ian Paxton. Straight out, and no messing with the programme on the knee – though it is comforting to have it there in case of the odd mental seizure.

TWO DIFFERENT EARS

Things have reached a stage where I now listen to sports commentators with, if you like, two different ears. One is taking in the event itself, the other is listening to how the commentator does his work, how he delivers his commentary, paces and projects himself. On radio you can hear some really first-rate sports commentators. A guy called Peter Jones, who does soccer matches, is a superb broadcaster and I get maybe twice the enjoyment listening to someone as good as he is.

Then there's the interviews – and that's a whole different technique. The first law of interviewing is that you must get the subject talking. If you say to a guy who's just come off the field: 'Well played, Joe. I thought your backs were brilliant,' you're inviting disaster because it's ten-to-one he will reply: 'Yes, they were.' So all you've done is waste ten seconds and then you have to start again.

The second law of interviewing is to work out in advance what would be interesting to the audience at home and try and set up the questions in such a way that the subject has room to give a decent answer. From my own experience of being interviewed as a player, I know how boring it can be if the questions are stupid or put badly. If I've just won the Grand Slam I don't want someone coming up to me and saying: 'Bill. You must be delighted.'

Everyone at home could answer that for me. What those people really want to know is how two of the lads managed to play on with a broken leg each and combine to score the winning try. That is what the interviewer should be asking.

When he puts his first question, the interviewer must also

Well, Scotland have just won the Grand Slam and it's over to Bill on my left for his unbiased comments.....

remember to give the name of the person he is talking to so that, from the start, no-one watching is left in any doubt. 'With me is Colin Deans,' he should say, loud and clear, 'captain of the Scotland team.'

Last year I interviewed Rob Andrew when he was wearing a Scotland jersey he'd just swapped with someone. 'Well, Rob,' I began – and we had anguished complaints from people who couldn't understand why I was interviewing a Scot. England had won 10–7 at Twickenham, so what did I think I was doing?

STUCK IN THE BOX

It's certainly tough up there in the press box. Once you're in, you're in – and there's no nipping out at half-time for a pee. So while I love the party atmosphere in the car park at Twickenham, I am currently barred from joining the champagne set for at least three reasons.

Firstly, I have to watch the liquid intake with unusual care just when the lunch parties are getting interesting. Secondly and thirdly, I have to keep my head clear, and in any case the BBC want us for broadcasting from about midday.

Apart from not having a drink before the game, the hardest part of the commentator's job is to fix his eyes on the monitor and keep them there until the final whistle. It's all right to have a look round, of course, and you need to know what your colleagues in the box – the match commentator, producer and engineer – are up to at all times so you can collaborate with them. You are wearing earphones and in one ear you can hear the commentator, in the other the producer. Suddenly a try is scored, and you know there will be an action replay. 'Right, run VT now,' says the producer. You're on.

Somehow you have to strike a happy medium between having something original and interesting to say when you are called in, but not something that is so original that only half the viewers can understand it. Also, you mustn't be boring. When you are called in to comment on a try-scoring move, it's no good merely repeating what the commentator has already said. If it is already established that Andrew passed to Halliday who passed to Smith who scored the try, it's not a comment just to say it all over again. What you need to do is find an angle, bring out something special in the play that led to the try. 'Look at this little break by Halliday,' you might say. 'He commits two defenders and that gives Smith the extra room to go over in the corner.'

My best commentary to date was one I delivered during the Scotland v France game in Paris in 1985. For about ten minutes we lost the sound altogether. 'Listen,' said a voice in my ear, 'the sound is so bad that we're cutting it off. So you're just in vision until we can improve it.' We had to carry on commentating, but to a distinctly limited audience. Afterwards the producer said that was the best spell of broadcasting he'd ever heard from me. I have decided to take it as a compliment.

MEN WITH WHISTLES

Let us consider the chief virtues which all referees must have. They must be impartial, good disciplinarians and, above all, be able to read the game in an open and enlightened way which makes it as enjoyable as possible for the players. At least, that's how I see it.

To take the first requirement – impartiality – this can be very hard to prove or disprove. If Fylde are playing Gloucester, for instance, and the referee for that afternoon has come from Walsall, who's to say he isn't going to be impartial? If there are no obvious geographical reasons for suspecting a ref in advance of favouring one side over another, it is perfectly reasonable to expect that he will give a fair, unbiased performance.

However, if you are on tour in Australia, as I was, and the referee runs on to the pitch wearing a pair of the home team's socks, then you are entitled to your doubts. At the first scrum we decided to test this man's loyalty further.

'Whose put-in is it?' we asked.

'Ours,' he replied.

At such times you are in what I might call South Sea Trouble. This is an affliction which strikes many a side touring the wonderful outposts of rugby in the Pacific. On the one hand, you don't always want to insist on bringing your own referee because it can seem patronizing or not justifiable depending on the circumstances of the country being visited. If their game is still in a fairly primitive state, then it may be OK, as it was for us when we played in Tonga. On the other hand, if you let them provide their own referee, you are quite possibly on to a loser, as the Lions found to their cost in Fiji.

I have mentioned this unfortunate defeat in an earlier chapter ('International Service') but, on reflection, I feel I have not paid sufficient tribute to some of the diabolical decisions made by their referee. At any level of the game something must be a bit out of order if one side gets three penalties and the opposition gets something between twenty and thirty. And when the suffering team (or villains) happen to be a touring side that have been playing together for four months, and so are even less likely to give away fouls than the majority of teams, then the imbalance becomes a real handicap and not something you can simply put down to misplaced enthusiasm.

South Sea Trouble can be found outside the Pacific region, but in an advanced rugby nation like Australia there's not a lot you can do about it. The authorities there would be deeply offended if you were to so much as suggest that their referees were not as impartial as those from the Mother Country. I just wish some refs would be a bit more subtle about it, that's all, and wear neutral gear and not chat to the opposition on first-name terms.

This is not to say for a moment that all foreign referees are bent. However, it does seem to be the case that the further from Europe you go as a player, the more you have to be prepared for some odd decisions. In South Africa the referees are, as you might expect, strict and not noted for their generosity to touring sides. At least I once had the consolation of getting an apology out of one of them.

I went over to ask why he hadn't ruled one of their players offside, and he immediately said: 'I am very sorry. I have made an accident.' (Which must be something like the Afrikaans for 'mistake'.)

He went on: 'I didn't think he was interfering with play.'

The player in question had just got hold of the ball and run seventy-five yards with it. I pointed this out to the ref and he agreed with me. It was a relief at the time because it proved that we were playing to the same set of rules after all!

REF IN THE POCKET

So much for impartiality. Let's look at discipline and how some referees assert their authority over the teams in their charge.

Discipline starts some while before the kick-off when the referee comes in to check the players' studs and make sure they are all legal. In Argentina, I remember, we got round this little difficulty by having two pairs of boots each, one pair perfectly acceptable which we showed the ref, and another pair which we put on when he had gone.

He came into the dressing-room, gave our boots a quick once-over and we tossed up. Then I asked him: 'How long is there to go before the kick-off?'

He looked at me. 'How long do you want?' he asked.

I'd never heard a referee ask that before! Whether it was said out of politeness or because he had a total disregard for time, I was never sure. What I do know is that we always kicked off late in Argentina.

One New Year's Day at Fylde I almost achieved my ambition of

Listen, Beaumont, I don't object to being carried under your arm but I **do** object to being bloody converted as a drop goal!

getting a referee in my pocket. Our team were a little the worse for wear before play began, but we weren't going to let that stop us. I came round on a peel at the back of the line-out and the referee was stood in the way. Acting on a rush of inspiration, I picked him up underneath my arm and carried him with me.

I don't think he was too upset. At least he kept his sense of humour, and I think all the players I know would rather have an official who allows the comic side of the game to come through every so often. In a friendly game, I once found myself disagreeing with a decision made by Peter Hughes, who was an international referee.

'Oh, bollocks, ref!' I said, a touch frustrated.

'We'll have no bollocks on a Sunday,' he said, and gave the other team an extra ten yards.

The ability to think fast like that is a great gift because it inclines players towards the referee and the job he has to do. Another man who uses a bit of chat to good effect is Clive Norling of Wales. If, for instance, you barge someone in the line-out early in the game he may not stop play but instead runs alongside you across the field and quietly says: 'I saw that.'

So now the player knows that the referee is looking out and he will have to think carefully about doing it again. That's what I call having a feel for the game. Those referees want to go out there and do their best to see that thirty guys enjoy themselves and have a good game of rugby. Nowadays, unfortunately, you tend to find a lot of referees with a more dictatorial attitude. 'Ah,' they think to themselves at the beginning of a game, 'now here I am with thirty players at my disposal, and I am going to *control* them.'

It's as though the rules of the game were more imortant than the game itself. They never were, and you won't find many players taking that view, which is why players value the more constructive kind of referee who lets play flow if he can but is not afraid to step in and sort out any funny business.

BEWITCHED, BERBIZIERED AND BEWILDERED

Every referee, no matter how quick or experienced, is bound to meet up with some bamboozling situations on the field which threaten to throw everything into confusion. In recent years I can think of two such incidents, both of them by coincidence involving Pierre Berbizier, the French scrum-half.

England were playing France at Twickenham in 1981, and both sides were going for the Championship. Marcus Rose, the England full-back, kicked the ball high into touch where it was caught by Dickie Jeeps in the RFU committee's section of the stand. As the England forwards stood around waiting for this ball to return to earth, Berbizier grabbed a replacement ball off a ball-boy and took a quick throw-in – from which the French scored.

I was furious and started raging at Alan Hosie, the referee. 'What the hell's going on here?' I wanted to know because the law states that you cannot take a quick throw-in with a replacement ball; you have to use the original one provided it can be recovered. However, the referee wouldn't change his mind and we had to accept it.

In my more sombre moments I wonder what would happen in a really big soccer match after the referee allowed a goal that was plainly illegal. Imagine Italy are playing Argentina in Buenos Aires in the Final of the World Cup. Italy are awarded a direct free-kick on the edge of the Argentinian penalty area and a quick-thinking, ambitious Italian nips up and scoops the ball over their goalkeeper and into the net before the defending side have a chance to form a wall and go through the usual rituals of defending their goal. The referee allows the goal, and Italy run out the winners by 1–0. Then what would happen, I wonder – to the referee, to the Italian team, to the World Cup....or even to world peace, come to think of it. We, on the other hand, had to be good sporting amateurs and put up with it. What's more, four points was the margin of France's victory in the match. *And* they won the Grand

Slam that year. No wonder we were choked.

The other incident was more mystifying, and I'm not sure if any single version of what should have happened has yet been accepted as correct. The year was 1986, and France were playing Scotland. The Scots kicked off and the ball went directly into touch. Usually what then happens is that the defending side asks either for the kick to be taken again or opts for a scrum on the halfway line. On that occasion

Look, ref — I'm not objecting to them scoring from a quick throw but shouldn't they wait until the game's actually started!

Berbizier took all the responsibility on himself and sent in a quick throw. Then, while the Scottish forwards were gently withdrawing towards the centre of the field, a raiding party of Frenchmen went flying down the wing. Referee David Burnett seemed poised to blow his whistle but did not, a Frenchman carried the ball over the Scottish goal-line and the try was given.

It all happened so fast, the cameras missed most of it. They had their shot of the ball going out of play from the kick-off....and then nothing until they caught up with the French raiders when they had about fifteen yards to go. At the time I was sat in the commentary position and my initial thoughts were on the lines of 'What the bloody hell's this?' My next thought was that the French move was probably all right because the touch-judge was running down the line with them and not signalling that he disapproved of anything.

I knew from the rules that you could take a quick throw-in from that position because the referee doesn't have to offer the play to the receiving side, so no decision is involved. Then I thought: 'But what about all those Frenchmen who were in offside positions – relative to where the ball went out – when the throw was taken?' Presumably the referee had decided that they were not interfering with play, so the move could be allowed to continue.

Nor was that the end of the possibilities. Another pundit was quick to say that play should have been stopped because the referee was not in a position to see whether the throw-in was taken properly, and I would not argue with that. The fact is, nine times out of ten the referee would have stopped play, on the instinctive grounds that the scene unrolling before his eyes was all so extraordinary, some of it must be illegal!

No, I would not have liked to be in David Burnett's shoes at that moment. But I feel I haven't heard the last of this incident. I'm waiting for it to turn up on *A Question of Sport* in the 'What Happened Next' part of the programme. When it does, I wonder what I'll say.

THE BEDSIDE XV

I have been approached, let us say, by a millionaire rugby fanatic. He wants me to select a touring side and manage it for him. I can have anyone I want, he says, from the whole history of the game.

I tell him I'll do it, but the players I select will have to be guys I've played with, preferably been on tour with, so we all know each other's little ways before we set off. If we aren't going to enjoy ourselves, it's not worth it. All right, he says, here's the team sheet. You pick your men. He passes me a used brown envelope and a chewed-up piece of pencil. Very smart, I think to myself, and wonder if he really is a millionaire or just one of those eccentric dreamers you meet in every clubhouse. Ah well, what does it matter. He's got to be eccentric, anyway, if he's willing to pick up the tab for the bunch of guys I'm going to give him. Here goes.

Next time, you ★⑥⊗◻※s, next time...

FULL-BACK

The best full-back I have ever played rugby with is Andy Irvine. J.P.R. Williams would normally run him close, but I have seldom played with J.P.R., almost always I've played against him, whereas I've been on two Lions tours with Andy. Therefore he gets my vote. I know he has had some anxious moments under the high ball, especially in internationals, but he is still my No. 1.

Andy was not only a great goal kicker (as he has proved against England on at least two occasions) but was probably the most exciting attacking full-back of all time.

On the social side he is great for team morale and wasn't the typical Scotsman with short arms and long pockets. His golf is pretty good as well, and there is always plenty of time on a rugby tour to fit in a round or two.

RIGHT-WING

John Carleton is a rare breed of player in this team in that he is still playing, and I should imagine that he will feature in England's World Cup hopes in 1987. He has been out in the wilderness for too long and if anyone doubts his try-scoring ability they just have to look back to his three tries in our Calcutta Cup game in 1980.

He also, along with Mike Slemen, made great travelling companions to and from internationals and squad sessions.

CENTRE-THREEQUARTERS

Two vacancies here and one of them goes to one of the great characters of British rugby, Ray Gravell, who was quoted as saying in South Africa in 1980: 'Get your first tackle in early, even if it's late!'

Ray is a great team man, although I'm not too sure about his musical taste. He was also a great tackler and a man who could be guaranteed to shore up the defence in the middle of the field.

As partner to Ray Gravell I have chosen a Scotsman, Jim Renwick, who has been the outstanding Scottish centre over the last decade, and I felt for both him and Andy Irvine that they didn't take part in Scotland's Grand Slam of 1984.

All the time I played against Jim he was a constant thorn in our side. There is a classic photo of me, Fran Cotton and Roger Uttley running at Jim who is the only man left to tackle us. Fran had given me the ball, I gave it to Roger, the ball went loose, Jim picked it up and put it into touch thirty yards away.

Andy Irvine commented on the photo: 'Jim Renwick versus three Englishmen. The odds must be even.'

LEFT-WING

Definitely Mike Slemen, who is probably the best rugby footballer I have ever had the pleasure to play alongside. People who have watched and admired him playing on TV must have noted not only his try-scoring ability but his ability to read a game so well with touch kicks and tackles. He could well have had a long and distinguished career as a full-back.

FLY-HALF

There's a good choice of players here and my choice goes to, believe it or not – for a Lancastrian to pick him he must be good – Alan Old. Who can forget his great performance for the North of England v All Blacks at Otley in 1979.

Far too many times he was wrongly dropped by England. He was a great tactical kicker and, not only that, he was also one of the great distributors of the ball. He was a great man to play against, as well, because he would usually start refereeing the game.

SCRUM-HALF

This has to be my old friend Steve Smith. At the start of my international career he was almost at the end of his first phase as an international. He was helped in 1979 by Des Seabrook, the Lancashire coach, to get his career under way again.

Steve always used to complain at scrummaging practice that he used to get his hands dirty and cold. When warming up by running round the pitch, it was impossible to get on the inside of him because he always took the shortest route – he was a genius at cutting corners. He always used to say: 'Don't cheat in training – because I invented it.'

He played some great rugby during the Grand Slam of 1980, always prompting and supporting his forwards. I think he got a try in both the Scotland and Ireland matches.

He did have to be helped out in the Welsh game that season, when he had his kick charged down by Alan Phillips which enabled Elgan Rees to score what we all thought were the winning points. It was the most difficult talk to a player I have ever had, choking back disappointment at the thought of losing the match, and at the same time motivating Steve. Thank goodness Dusty Hare kicked the winning penalty two minutes later.

PROP

I might as well tell you now, the front row is going to be the Lions front row in New Zealand in 1977 – Fran Cotton, Peter Wheeler, Graham Price. Let's begin with Cotton.

As a twenty-year-old and a member of the Lancashire squad, I was lucky to come under the influence of the greatest prop forward to play in the last decade. Not only was he an outstanding ball-player, a legacy of his Rugby League upbringing, he was good enough to play both loose and tight head at international level.

I had the pleasure to pack behind him in the scrum on many occasions and whilst I would not put the blame for my cauliflower ears on him, we ended up going forward more times than backwards in the scrum, largely due to Fran.

HOOKER

Bar three internationals, Peter Wheeler was the hooker I always played with, either with England or the British Lions. He was the only hooker who could make me seem half-reasonable in the lineout. He was simply the best; how he could have been ignored for the Lions tour to New Zealand in 1983 is beyond me.

In modern-day rugby the art of the hooker is disappearing fast; Wheeler was a craftsman. He is also a pretty good golfer and has been known to chip into the hole from way off the green, as he did once in Fiji. He then took half an hour filming it for posterity. He did once look a little worried playing in South Africa behind Fran and myself. Fran found a dead snake on the course and returned to the hole we had just played and put the snake in the hole. Fran and I had great delight in watching Peter pick his ball from the hole.

72

PROP

The quietest member of the front row, and a member of the famous Pontypool front row, Graham Price was, like Fran Cotton, one of the most mobile props ever to play international rugby. He was also a more than useful lineout jumper, often frustrating me by intercepting my low throw. I played behind Pricey in seven Lions Tests, and in every one of them he had the upper hand. He also complained to me in all of them that there wasn't enough weight coming through from the second row.

SECOND ROW

Without a doubt Moss Keane would get my vote here, especially if we were a touring side. He always had a habit (I don't know whether it's an old Irish speciality) of spitting on his hands, clenching his fist and then saying: 'I'll bust you.' He used to do this to me at kick-offs before England v Ireland matches, but we would both be smiling. It shows that even at the highest level opponents can still be great friends. He was probably the most awkward opponent I ever played against, and I can remember being on a few receiving ends from him in Dublin.

Moss's partner in the second row would be my old England partner Maurice Colclough. I first came across Maurice when he was a student at Liverpool University. In those days he looked the typical student – ex-RAF coat, shoulder-length hair, carrying his rugby kit in a plastic bag. Later he became something of a business entrepreneur, with interests in Swansea and Angouleme. He played in France for many years after arriving in Angouleme on holiday and playing in a club trial match, then staying on running bars, hire boats, etc. Sharing a room with him was akin to being his business secretary.

In 1980 on the Lions Tour he was simply outstanding, dominating the lineouts against much bigger opponents, while his scrummaging prowess was something to behold.

Maurice was one amongst many great second-rows I have played with and against but I would have to have him in my team.

BACK-ROW
WING FORWARDS

To my mind Tony Neary was the best. To think, he went on two Lions tours and only played in one Test match. He could do simply everything, and it is quite right that he is England's most capped player. What a pity he missed out in 1977 and 1978 from England selection.

He could dominate the tail of a lineout and still be the best support player I have seen, along with Fran Cotton. I had the benefit of learning such a lot from these two great players when I was a young lad in the Lancashire squad. You have only to ask some of the great players he played against, such as Jean-Pierre Rives and Graham Mourie, to find out what a great player he was.

Jean-Pierre Rives would be my other wing forward in the team. A man who captained France over thirty times has to be respected. He was also a great host, and when playing over in Paris you only had to mention his name and you could get into any nightclub or restaurant.

Many of his critics used to complain about him trying to referee matches, but I can understand his frustration at always having to be refereed by English-speaking refs. He also was prone to getting cut around the head and invariably ended up with blood all over the place, looking as though tomato ketchup had been poured over his head. But you would have to go a long way to find a player who was more courageous and I would like people to remember him at the start of his career rather than the frustrated player he became.

He and I played in many Barbarian and Invitation teams, and he could always be guaranteed to give 100 per cent in every game.

NUMBER 8

This is Andy Ripley, one of the last of the old Corinthians, a magnificent athlete who, if he had been coached as a young player, would have ended up as one of the all-time greats. I always felt that he had a raw deal regarding England selection; too often people would criticize his faults, but in no way should these have detracted from his attributes. His domination at the back of the lineout and his explosive pace should have been better utilized.

I would make him the team's fitness trainer, because it didn't matter how fit anyone else got, he would still be only at about half Rippers's level. When he took training sessons, he would often say: 'If you want to do it, OK. If you don't want to do it, that's also OK by me.'

IN CONCLUSION

Here, to recap, is the team: A.R. Irvine; J.Carleton, R.W.R. Gravell, J.M. Renwick, M.A.C. Slemen; A.G.B. Old, S.J. Smith; G. Price, P.J. Wheeler, F.E. Cotton, M.I. Keane, M.J. Colclough, A. Neary, A.G. Ripley, J-P. Rives.

I reckon that's a pretty handy bunch of men. As team manager I can see my chief task will be to keep them on the straight and narrow and make sure they turn up fit for all our matches. I have just heard, by the way, from our wealthy patron and sponsor that we begin the tour with a month's acclimatization in Chicago, and then we play the Bears. At which game he didn't say. Should be interesting.

IF IT'S SPRING WE MUST BE AT THE SEVENS

Sevens is a great game for players *and* watchers. If you are a watcher the two big events to go to are the Middlesex Sevens at Twickenham and the Scottish Sevens. For the Scots this is not a single tournament but a way of life which every year overtakes the Border strongholds of rugby from March to April.

The venues could hardly be more different. Twickenham, whatever the official view might lead you to believe, is a gigantic party held in the shadows of the huge and familiar grandstands and drawing rugby nuts from a whole lot further afield than the boundaries of Middlesex, that shadowy county which governments have ignored and now only exists for the important things in life, e.g. rugby and cricket. Twickenham is where the signs warn you that no-one carrying alcohol will be allowed into the ground – and while you are stood there reading the sign, a guy walks past with a barrel of beer strapped to his back. Next to him comes his mate holding the gas cylinder. In they go, into the arena, which soon will be witnessing the day's first streaker.

The last time I was at the Middlesex Sevens we had a good half-dozen streakers during the day; the only trouble was, they were all blokes! That Erika Roe may have started something, but now I'm wondering precisely what it was she started. It's not as if the ground was bathed in spring sunshine, that year it was distinctly chilly. I would have thought there was nothing worse than being a goose-pimpled exhibitionist, particularly if you've been marched off by the police and now you've been separated from your clothes for ten minutes, fifteen minutes, twenty....

In Scotland it's far too cold for that kind of frivolity. In any case, the

Wull, Tam, this wan will nae streak again

Scots take their Sevens seriously, to the extent that they play no fifteen-a-side matches in April. Instead, the leading clubs like Hawick, Kelso, Gala, Jedforest, Selkirk and others stage a series of Sevens at their various grounds, and victory in these tournaments is counted by every club as a major part of the season's achievement.

The venues there are much more intimate than at Twickenham, and the view will be of rolling hills rather than tiers of seats and giant sloping roofs. In the Border country people who like watching their rugby from a high vantage-point must come early and claim a place on the branch of a tree. Meanwhile, down on the ground, it's a fast and furious game which largely consists of hard-running moves punctuated more by try-scoring bursts than by scrums and line-outs. Such is the pace, a player who has already run down his end-of-season training too severely can find himself in trouble. Certainly, the best time to take a rest is immediately someone on your side makes a break for the line from a defensive position. Then you've only got to amble up to the halfway line and enjoy a good long gasp for air while one of your team-mates takes the conversion. If the try-scorer is an opponent then it's not so funny, either from the points aspect or from the R & R (rest and recuperation) because you have to trail all the way back to your try-line, by which time their kicker is waiting to start his run-up and you've hardly got the chance even for a good gob.

In 1976 I got through to a Scottish semi-final while playing for a Barbarians VII, and I can vouch for the speed at which things happen. When the scrum consists of only three forwards, each must take on a specialist role as well as being prepared to run about halfway to the Moon and back. One forward has to be the hooker, and of the others one is usually a ball-player and one is a ball-winner. These highly tuned men often come from elsewhere in the eight-man scrum to perform their athletic duties (you won't find many props built like martello towers in the seven-a-side game).

After you have laboured manfully for a while at Sevens, but most of it has been in vain, you begin to appreciate that there is a distinct art to the game. Already you have noticed that the majority of your opponents look much more lively and content than you do. You have also worked out why. It is because they are winning. Yes, quite, you don't need a degree in sports psychology to work that out. The point is…. *why* are they winning? At about the sixth time of asking, the coin finally clatters into position: they are winning, and therefore look more lively and content than you do – because they've *got the ball.*

Having, and keeping, the ball is central to winning anything at Sevens. Once you have understood this, and have begun to practise it, you are on your way. I can offer no finer proof of this than a Sevens match I once played in for Fylde. Remember: possession is all. This is how it went.

We kicked off. They caught the ball, kept it and scored. They converted it, and we kicked off for the second time. The same thing happened again, and, after one or two minor breaks and diversions, again. Half-time arrived, we hadn't touched the ball and they were leading 18–0.

One of the lads said to me during the break: 'Ey, Bill. This could be a cricket score.'

I said: 'No it won't.'

'Why's that?' he asked.

'Because,' I told him, 'it's their turn to kick off next.'

And so it turned out. In the second half the reverse happened and we scored three times. At full-time the score was 18–18 and we had to play extra-time to sort it out.

Now, there must be a way of not kicking it to them in the first place….

Right...lads.....we'll...
..get....them....in.....
the...second.....half...
... eh...lads ?...
.... lads ?.....

THE CAPTAIN

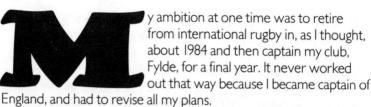

My ambition at one time was to retire from international rugby in, as I thought, about 1984 and then captain my club, Fylde, for a final year. It never worked out that way because I became captain of England, and had to revise all my plans.

Before I was appointed I had captained club teams every so often, but never on an official basis. Suddenly I was in charge of the national side, and our first fixture in the Five Nations Championship was France away – the Grand Slam champions. Despite the honour of it all, I also had a certain feeling of 'Why me?' Then, at the Parc des Princes, amid

An England captain is supposed to _dress_ for dinner, Beaumont!

all that amazing French uproar, we were ahead 6–3 and in with a real chance. We held that narrow lead for a long time before they hit us with two super tries in the closing minutes; the final score was 15–6.

I came away from Paris with an odd mixture of feelings. We had played well, we had been unlucky with injuries, and we had lost. I had also experienced one of the great, great moments of my life, leading the England team into that bellowing arena. When I return there now, I can still sense the extraordinary thrill of '78.

The next match was the other hard one of the year – Wales at home. We again lost narrowly and I began to think: 'Here we go – wooden spoon again.' Then we beat Scotland 15–0 at Murrayfield, and Ireland 15–9 in our last game. I felt at last we were pulling ourselves out of the pit; in fact, by previous standards it had been a respectable season. The following year we got one win and one draw; Ireland beat us, and Wales murdered us 27–3 – one further nail in the coffin of my secret ambition to win in Cardiff. We never made it in my time. In all I led England in twenty games, but after 1979 I wouldn't have been surprised if someone else had been given the job. The next year we won everything.

From the beginning I had my doubts and worries. Not so much about what we would do on the field, more about how I would be able to motivate people and handle the team talks. I was well aware that several guys in the team had much more experience of captaining teams than I had. There was also the ceremonial side. I hadn't a clue about making speeches at dinners, and doing all the ambassadorial stuff that is also the captain's lot.

In the end I decided that the ceremonial side would somehow have to take care of itself. My chief aim would be to lead the team by personal example, both on the training field and in our matches. That way the other guys would see that the captain was getting stuck in and they would feel encouraged to follow suit. Provided they were happy with the role they had been given to play in the match, and provided also we had done our homework on the opposition and pre-planned as much as we could, we should be well placed to give of our best. A captain can only do so much; beyond a certain stage he has to rely on his players.

Before that first match in Paris, we knew we would be faced by a massive French pack, and we were discussing our tactics. Mike Burton, one of our props, had firm ideas on the subject.

'There's only one thing we can do,' he said, 'and that's put the ball in quickly and get it away. We don't want to mess around in the scrum with these guys.'

To me that didn't sound right. And now that I was captain, it was up to me to assert my feelings and get the forwards doing what I thought best. I said: 'Look, it doesn't matter if it happens in the first scrum or the twentieth, eventually we are going to have to take them on. We might as well do it from the start.'

That was how we played it, and we did pretty well for ball. We were unlucky to lose two players through injury, and then Robin Cowling dislocated a shoulder. We were out of substitutes, and he managed, remarkably, to stay on the field until the final whistle. At the end of it, battered and defeated though we were, I knew we had done the right thing to stand up to them from the outset, and give them a battle to remember. I still see my old French cronies from that time, and we have a great feeling of warmth for each other. They know we came close to beating them.

EASIER FOR FORWARDS

Does it matter where the captain plays? I think it does. On the field of play it is easier for a forward to get warmed up and become involved with the spirit of the game. From the first whistle the forwards are steaming round with the ball, or in close pursuit of it; they are in physical contact with the opposition for the whole game, and so they are easier for a captain to direct.

The scrum-half is a crucial figure because he is the link-man between the forwards and the backs. He puts the ball in at the scrums; receives it from the lineout and feeds it out to the quick men. For these reasons a lot of scrum-halves are made captain. To me, however, it makes more sense if the captain is a forward because he will always be in the middle of the action. This can be a great

85

advantage if used properly. The great models I looked to were players like Eric Evans and Willie John McBride. They led from the front and by their style of play they won the support of the rest of the team.

On a tour the captain has very much the same problems as he faces at home, but in an extended form. To some degree it is a twenty-four-hour job because he has to be concerned with the well-being of all the players around the clock. It is no good shoving off to the bar with the main mob and leaving any others to get on with it by themselves. Some players are natural loners and don't want to be in a crowd all the time or be chivvied about. The captain must respect this, and find time to make sure that all the players are happy in their own way.

This applies in particular to the guys who aren't getting a game. The captain has to keep them informed and involved, to help them appreciate that they have a role to play as a member of the team even if they aren't being chosen for the Test side.

On a more positive note, the captain should try to ensure that the team enjoy themselves. Tours can be lengthy and difficult, and the captain should be flexible and not dogmatic, prepared to listen to other people's suggestions. If the guys would rather play golf in the morning and train in the afternoon, fine, let them do it that way. If it has already been arranged the other way round, change it. Team spirit is more important than giving the captain an easy time.

Altogether, I was captain of England for four and a half years. People now remember me as the captain of the Grand Slam side, and I am grateful for that. I am also aware that a captain is judged by the team's results, and not so much by how they played. We beat Wales in 1980, as part of our winning campaign, but we only beat them by three penalties to two tries. People are inclined to forget that. I am not complaining.

A QUESTION OF RUGBY

I was still playing rugby when I began appearing as a panellist in *A Question of Sport*. That was five years ago, and now there are young people watching the programme who don't know me as a former player; to them I am the guy who never gets his rugby questions right.

This horrible reputation took root when Willie Carson knew the answer to my rugby question and I didn't. If the ground could have opened up in front of me, I would gladly have jumped inside.

The producer enjoyed my embarrassment so much that, ever since, the researchers have been ferreting out the most obscure rugby questions for me and the most obscure soccer questions for Emlyn Hughes. Compared with the questions they throw at us, the guest panellists are let off lightly. Emlyn and I are the scapegoats – the men they love to see struggling.

One of my more long-drawn-out blunders had to do with the Russell Cargill Trophy. The what? The Russell Cargill Trophy. If you don't know, and I didn't, it's what your team get if they win the Middlesex Sevens. I was asked to name the current holders and, not knowing what the trophy was, failed to score.

Next year David Coleman said: 'Bill, you know what the Russell Cargill Trophy is?'

'Yes,' I said, all bright and smart, 'it's for the Middlesex Sevens. Wasps won it last year'.

'Yes,' said David, 'and who were runners-up?'

See, if I'd kept my mouth shut, he'd have asked me who won it. But I didn't. So he didn't. And I got it wrong. It caused a slight stir at the time. People in the street were saying: 'Hmm. Must be a bit of a dummer, that bloke. Doesn't know who were the runners-up for the Russell Cargill Trophy. Or anything else about rugby'.

That Bill Hughes and Emlyn Beaumont—They always get it wrong

SEX PROBLEMS

I have had a lot of trouble with the Mystery Guest. More precisely, with the sex of the Mystery Guest. I thought Ann Hobbs was Jim Watt, and mistook Steve Cram for a woman. My wife had a quiet word with me. 'Look at their feet,' she said. 'You can tell by the size of their feet.'

It wasn't a bad piece of advice. Not perfect, mind you; not infallible as I have since proved on more than one occasion.

Happily though, I had no trouble sexing Laurent Pardo. The trouble was, he is a French rugby player and I couldn't think of his name. The lads gave me a lot of stick for that, but it was a complete mental block, that's all. Anyone can have them.

Then, last year – this was really evil – the researchers found a highly obscure photograph of Nigel Melville and put it on the pictureboard. I didn't recognize it. Later, I discovered that even his parents didn't recognize it, and I have been using them ever since to excuse myself. Nigel wasn't offended, fortunately. It's just that now, whenever we meet, he says: 'Hello, I'm Nigel Melville.'

I should have stuck to cricket. I do quite well with cricket questions, in fact I now think of myself as a frustrated cricketer. In my boyhood dreams I batted for England. Nothing wrong with that. In other dreams I played football for Blackburn Rovers, but cricket was the main attraction. And no wonder. When cricketers go on tour they go to brilliant sunny places where it's beautiful and warm. We, on the other hand, get New Zealand in winter. Sixteen weeks of pouring rain and never a sight of the sun.

That's rugby for you. What a game.